The Power of Positivity for Kids

How to Use Positive Thoughts for Kids to Grow a Positive Mind

Frank Dixon

from various sources. Please consult a licensed professional before attempting any techniques outlined in this book.

By reading this document, the reader agrees that under no circumstances is the author responsible for any losses, direct or indirect, that are incurred as a result of the use of the information contained within this document, including, but not limited to, errors, omissions, or inaccuracies.

Before we begin, I have something special waiting for you. An action-packed 1 page printout with a few quick & easy tips taken from this book that you can start using today to become a better parent right now!

It's my gift to you, free of cost. Think of it as my way of saying thank you to you for purchasing this book.

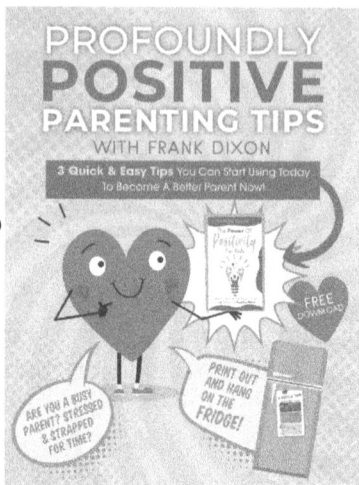

Claim your download of Profoundly Positive Parenting with Frank Dixon by scanning the QR code below and join my mailing list.

Sign up below to grab your free copy, print it out and hang it on the fridge!

Sign Up By Scanning The QR Code With Your Phone's Camera To Be Redirected To A Page To Enter Your Email And Receive INSTANT Access To Your Download

Before we jump in, I'd like to express my gratitude. I know this mustn't be the first book you came across and yet you still decided to give it a read. There are numerous courses and guides you could have picked instead that promise to make you an ideal and well-rounded parent while raising your children to be the best they can be.

But for some reason, mine stood out from the rest and this makes me the happiest person on the planet right now. If you stick with it, I promise this will be a worthwhile read.

In the pages that follow, you're going to learn the best parenting skills so that your child can grow to become the best version of themselves and in doing so experience a meaningful understanding of what it means to be an effective parent.

Notable Quotes About Parenting

"Children Must Be Taught How To Think, Not What To Think."

— Margaret Mead

"It's easier to build strong children than to fix broken men [or women]."

- Frederick Douglass

"Truly great friends are hard to find, difficult to leave, and impossible to forget."

— George Randolf

"Nothing in life is to be feared, it is only to be understood. Now is the time to understand more, so that we may fear less."

— Scientist Marie Curie

Table of Contents

Introduction

When children turn three, they begin to identify emotions they encounter in different situations. They can differentiate between good and bad times and what emotions accompany them. For instance, if they are being scolded, it accompanies anger and sadness. If there is a birthday party, it accompanies happiness and laughter. When they turn six, they become more aware of the connection between their feelings and thinking. By the time they turn seven, they can understand that people have the power to interpret the same situation in different ways.

According to a recent study, researchers looked at how the understanding of children between the ages of five and 10 about thinking positively changes with the developmental changes they go through (Bamford & Lagattuta, 2011). It also looked at whether this affected a child's emotional response or not.

During the experiment, 90 children were put in three groups based on their age. The first group had children aged five and six. The second group had children aged seven and eight. The third group had children aged nine and also 10. All the groups were introduced to three pairs of characters that went through a positive, negative, and neutral experience. In the first scenario, the character got a new pet; in the second, the character broke their arm while playing; and in the third, the character met a new teacher.

One character within each pair framed the event in a positive light and the other in a negative light. For instance, one of the characters from the pair that broke their arm interpreted the situation positively as they got others to sign their cast, whereas the other character from the same pair characterized the situation negatively, thinking how uncomfortable the cast will be.

The children taking part were then asked to report on the characters' feelings. Did the characters feel good about what happened? Why did they feel a certain way? The children were further questioned about why they thought one character felt good and the other didn't. Their explanations were characterized as either situation or mental explanations, meaning that the majority of them thought that the situation triggered a certain emotion (situation), or the characters' thoughts, preferences, and desires caused the emotions (mental).

In all three groups, children identified positive thinking and negative thinking based on the experiences the character had. The third group seemed more aware of how thoughts can be reframed. They were aware that reframing an event in the mind can either positively or negatively affect an individual's emotional experience. However, regardless of their age, all children believed that in negative situations, thinking positively wasn't enough to make one feel better. Now, although many would disagree with this notion, what the study provided was an insight into how the children were being raised by their parents. It wasn't the child's level of optimism and hope that was revealed but that of their parents.

The findings suggested that parents have to play an important role to teach children how to use positive thinking when things are tough and to model behavior accordingly. The findings revealed that when children found themselves—or the characters, in this case—in trouble, they didn't think that positive thinking would help them get out of it. They lacked the hindsight to look at the bright side.

The researchers also concluded that children as young as five had already begun to develop skills that enabled them to differentiate between positive and negative reframing and how it can change an individual's response to any situation. Researchers believe that training children to become positive and change their pessimistic thinking into positive thinking can yield great, long-term benefits for them. This can help them not only overcome difficult times but also alleviate stress in the long run, which happens to be the crux of most problems these days. Reframing thoughts to overcome negative situations is an essential life skill to nurture in children, and many other studies prove this.

If you would like to instill a positive outlook in your child's life, too, then give them the essential tools they need to combat negative thinking. This guide can be a great start to understand what you must do to begin.

Chapter 1:

Positivity and Its Growing

Need Among Kids

It seems the world has taken a nosedive into the pits of negativity given the recent pandemic. With adolescents and teenagers unable to cope with the mental turmoil it comes with, it can be difficult for them to see the positive side of things. Negativity surrounds them. From news to events that affect all of us differently, it is hard to not succumb to a pessimistic mindset. Many teenagers who should have been living their best lives right now are in their homes, isolated and by themselves. They need more light, more hope, and positivity. If we look at the statistical data from the Centers for Disease Control and Prevention (CDC), it further confirms the analysis. There has been a rise in mental disorders among children of all ages—even as little as three. Nearly, 7.4% of children from ages three to a teen of 17 have a diagnosed mental disorder. Around 7.1% of them suffer from anxiety, and 3.2% (nearly 1.9 million) children have diagnosed depression (Ghandour et al., 2019). Some conditions like anxiety and depression occur simultaneously, too, which only makes matters worse.

To alleviate their growing stress and anxiety, many children indulge in self-harming activities such as substance abuse, smoking, and alcohol. According to research, by 12th grade, two-thirds of students have tried alcohol at least once (Johnston et al., 2003). Half of the ninth graders have reported using and having marijuana (The Partnership for Drug-Free Kids, 2014). Shockingly, four of the 10 students in 12th grade have tried cigarettes (Grunbaum et al., 2000).

Such practices combined with negative thoughts can have a detrimental effect on their mental stability and lead to thoughts about suicide. Constant stress and anxiety about what the future holds also diminishes their self-confidence and self-worth. They feel unprepared to deal with the daily stresses of life and unfortunately have no one to turn to. Thus, we see the growing need for something positive!

A positive attitude or mindset refers to viewing oneself positively. It also includes looking at others with a progressive and hopeful perspective. It doesn't mean that you ignore the negativity. Rather, it means to perceive situations, no matter how dark they seem, in a constructive manner.

Thus, nurturing a hopeful and constructive viewpoint in a child's life becomes essential. It uplifts their confidence in their abilities and skills. It prepares them to deal with any crisis life throws at them. It comforts them in difficult times. It keeps them hoping for the best when all hope is lost.

For a parent to do that, the first thing you must do is understand your child's behavior. Do they seem positive or pessimistic about things? Are they quick to give up or continue trying? Do they embrace challenges with confidence or not?

For many, it can be a Herculean task, as children can be quite unpredictable. However, if we look closer, the majority of the habits they develop are a reflection of us. They do as they see us doing. However, this isn't enough. Sometimes, their interpretation of a certain behavior can be misguided. For example, they can misinterpret temporary sadness as hopelessness. Similarly, they can misjudge happiness as a constant state and not be able to comprehend their emotions when they experience the opposite. That being said, their emotions and feelings shouldn't go unnoticed—especially when they are negative. If a child is being stubborn for no reason, this behavior shouldn't be promoted or ignored as childishness. If left untreated, it can blossom into an undesirable trait.

To identify if they have a positive or negative approach toward life, below are a few signs to confirm.

Does your child:

- Feel confident in their abilities or compare themselves with others?

- Seem happy and spirited or depressed and discouraged?

- Act responsible or behave stubbornly over silly things?

- Mingles with friends and family or prefers to stay in their room alone?

- Show good academic performance or display no efforts to improve?

- Show gratitude over what they have or receive or unpleasant with the gifts they receive?

- Seem motivated and optimistic about the future or demotivated and disheartened about it?

If you notice them being optimistic, hopeful, and happy with who they are and an eagerness to improve, then they have a positive mindset. If they seem more disheartened with every failure or setback, don't make any efforts to improve their performance, and have a generally negative outlook toward life, then they have a negative mindset.

Once you understand their approach, behaviors, and actions, you will be in a better position to help them. Life is ruthless, and it won't spare your child unless they have the guts to stand for themselves and be assertive. As adults, we know this, and nothing breaks our hearts more than the fact that we feel our child is too vulnerable for the world. Thankfully, a positive mindset can be nurtured.

The benefits of positive thinking for children are many. For starters, it makes them more resilient. Resilience is the ability to easily bounce back after experiencing a setback or failure. It makes one feel more in control, tough, and prepared to handle any situation without losing their optimism and nerves. When a positive mindset fosters resilience, a child feels more confident in managing life's inevitable disappointments like not getting on the school soccer team, getting dumped by their partner, bad grades, or rejection from their chosen college or job. A study involving 5,600 teenagers suggests that children that are trained to think optimistically are less likely to suffer from depression or anxiety later in their lives (Patton et al., 2011). They learn to look past their failures and continue to give life their best shot.

A positive outlook toward life also improves overall health. Some studies connect positivity with improved immune functioning (Segerstrom & Miller, 2004). A positive mindset prevents stress which keeps blood pressure and heart rate in control. Even when one experiences negative emotions, the body doesn't overpower the system with adrenaline or trigger the fight-or-flight response. This prevents an individual from making hasty or untimely decisions. Positivity promotes health and manages stress and anxiety.

A positive mindset also prompts school-age children to take risks and try new things. It encourages students to explore and discover new passions and talents. It also has a constructive impact on learning. During one study, researchers at Stanford University School of

Medicine studied 240 students aged from the ages of seven to 10 (Chen et al., 2018). They found that children with a positive mindset were better at math and problem solving. They also had improved memory, suggesting that their brain worked at a faster rate than those who lacked an initiative mindset. Improved memory means better comprehension and recall which aids in exams and other skill-building practices.

A positive attitude also boosts a child's self-esteem. It makes them feel comfortable in their skin. They feel grateful for who they are and what they are ultimately capable of. Children with a positive mindset know that they can improve in areas that need work and become a master of all things. Positivity rewires their subconscious by embedding positive thoughts and ideas about themselves and others which helps them excel in everything they set their mind to.

Positive people also tend to be happier than those who aren't positive. Studies show that positive people are less likely to engage in self-harming behaviors and practices. They remain content with what they have and don't try to control every aspect of their lives. The research that provided evidence studied over 275,000 individuals and determined whether happiness causes success or success causes happiness (Lyubomirsky et al., 2005). At first, data provided the researchers with a "chicken-and-egg" situation, but later, longitudinal data confirmed that happiness was a primary factor for success. Participants that seemed happy with where they were in their lives engaged in less risky behaviors like smoking, substance abuse, alcohol, or unhealthy eating.

All of these studies are predictive of how crucial a positive mindset is in a child's life. Therefore, as parents, it is on us whether we succeed in cultivating one in them or not. To help you get started, the following chapters present the necessary steps you need to take to raise a child with a positive mindset.

Chapter 2:

Practice What You Preach

Many people our age remember *Jaws* as the greatest movie of its time. We were all fascinated by the amazingness of it—the script, thrill, and the sharks, of course, had many never return to the open waters for months. However, not many people remember a scene portraying a bond between the child and the parent that left such a strong impression.

Sheriff Brody and his son are sitting at the dinner table. As the Sheriff's wife sets the table, Brody sits at the head of it, staring into the distance, unaware of his son's presence or actions. His son, carefully watching his every move and mimicking it, may not seem like a scene worth remembering, but it goes on to show how much our children look up to us, even when we aren't noticing. When the Sheriff sips his drink, so does the child. When the Sheriff folds his hands, his son follows the same. Every movement the Sheriff makes is imitated by the little one until the Sheriff realizes and makes playful movements for his son to copy (Spielberg, 1975).

This goes on to suggest that sometimes we forget that the role models our children need in their lives are the ones we look at in the mirror every day. It is us—their very guide and mentor. We are their best friend and guardian—the people they look up to for everything. Our actions and behaviors don't go unnoticed. They are studied and mimicked; they turn into lifelong habits. They become a reflection of who our children grow up to be.

That being said, we have to be extra cautious with what we have to offer. Do you think you make an ideal role model for your child? Do you want them to follow in your path? Do you want them to grow up just like you?

Therefore, for them to cultivate a positive mindset, you have to develop one in yourself. To set the right example and help them follow in your footsteps, you have to be optimistic about who you are. Your child should see you grasping opportunities with both hands. They should see you having strong and loving interpersonal relationships with everyone. They should see you embracing and acknowledging negative emotions and still keeping a smile on your face. If you can succeed in doing so, you can remain hopeful that your child will pick up the same tastes and develop the same habits.

Becoming a role model isn't as easy as it sounds. It starts with having a close and honest look at your strengths and weaknesses and how you model them. It involves introspecting how you live your life and whether you want to create a similar one for your young one or not. This kind of self-analysis can be uncomfortable, as you are likely going to come across some undesirable traits within yourself. However, since the well-being of your child is at stake, you may want to take the leap and change for the better.

Like most parents, it is understandable that you want your child to grow in a healthy and happy environment where everyone shows respect and consideration for one another, but remember: Good habits aren't taught; they are developed through positive experiences. Before we talk about how parents can use their behaviors and actions to foster positive thinking, let's quickly review some of the most important characteristics of a role model.

What Does a Role Model Look Like?

A role model is someone whose actions and behaviors others like to imitate. They have positive habits that inspire others. They have the confidence and control to transform their bad habits into constructive ones—if any. They are admired for their personality and charisma. People are drawn to them naturally and like to follow in their footsteps. They set the right examples for others and tell them, through their behavior, what they should and shouldn't do.

Children with strong parental role models have a greater chance of developing the same traits and talents their parents have. They have a better chance of adopting the same positive mindset and lifestyle. What are these lifestyle traits and talents that they possess? Let's find out!

High Morals

A role model parent has high morals. According to research by developmental psychologist Marilyn Price-Mitchell, children show respect toward those who practice what they preach, meaning they live the life they claim to live (Howe, 2018). Role models are honest, supportive of worthy causes, and willing to act on the things they believe in. They have strong core values and standards for themselves and others. They are ethically responsible and accountable for their actions at all times.

Respectful

Role models may be influential, but they show respect and consideration toward others. They treat all those above or below them with the level of respect that they deserve. They are democratic, selfless, and unprejudiced when it comes to making decisions or forming judgments about someone. These skills make them admirable among their friends, peers, and family.

Optimistic and Creative

Role models have a positive mindset. They are often upbeat and optimistic about life. They inspire creativity and enthusiasm in others. Role models see the bright side of things in difficult times and can come up with creative solutions to resolve their problems.

Humble

Humility is another important characteristic of a role model parent. They are accepting of others. Role models also have a willingness to improve, admit, and correct themselves where needed. They learn from their mistakes and take responsibility for them.

Empathizing

Ideal role models have an empathetic heart. They don't go offering unsolicited advice to everyone they meet. They are understanding and kind. They are responsive and effective listeners. Role models understand what a person is going through and offer comfort that's free of any bias or judgment.

Curiosity

Role models have a curious mind. They love to explore and learn about new things. They are fans of lifelong learning and show a willingness to try new things and skills despite their age. When such people parent children, they raise curious individuals who are ready to take risks and try new things. They raise adults who can step out of their comfort zones and embrace uncertainty.

How Becoming a Role Model Sets the Perfect Example to Foster Positivity

Becoming a role model for your child can help foster a positive mind. You can do so by spending time with them and talking about your failures and successes. This will teach them how to be prepared for any unpredictability and be flexible. They also get to connect with you and learn about your childhood and teen struggles, and hopefully, they can learn a lot from you.

You can also help them set short-term and long-term goals. Such topics can be great conversation starters. Setting goals together helps them align their actions with their end goals and use their resources, like time and money, wisely. Additionally, if they see you achieving your goals and objectives, they will be motivated to do the same.

They should also see you being compassionate and kind toward your family, relatives, and friends. They should see you respecting others and showing consideration. Your house should fuel the right kind of behavior and energy. It should serve as a place for your children to relax, be open, and be communicative with one another. They should feel included, not ignored. They should feel validated and not neglected. The type of relationship they have with you is the kind of relationship they will seek from others. If there is negativity and discouragement, they will seek out partners that are toxic and appreciative. Therefore, to prevent this from happening, here's what you can do:

- Help them identify the qualities they admire in a role model. Take a sheet of paper and ask them what they think makes an inspiring role model.

- Once they have a list, find someone that has those traits and qualities. It can be a relative, teacher, or someone from your community. Take them to meet that person and see how they feel influenced by them.

- Finally, try to model the same qualities in yourself; at the end of the day, they learn the most from you.

Chapter 3:

Reframe Negative Thoughts Into Positive Ones

As parents, we are quick to point out any negative behavior or action in our children. However, sometimes, it is our internal dialogue that needs to be called out. It is what holds us back from unlocking our true potential. It is what tells us that we aren't good enough, worthy enough of the good things, or don't have what it takes to be successful. Countering this critic should be your primary goal.

Children can develop similar thinking, too. It can affect their confidence, mental being, and emotional well-being. It can scare them, make them question their abilities, and refrain from trying anything remotely challenging. If left to nurture, their inner critic can dominate all their actions and reactions and prevent them from achieving greatness in life.

Therefore, the second step to cultivate a positive mindset in adolescents and teenagers is to help them reframe such negative thoughts with positive ones. It can begin with a simple shift such as substituting some words with better words like describing laziness as "lack of interest" in something or describing something difficult as "not being fully prepared," etc. Rephrasing sentences like these when children come up to you with their worries and troubles can help them look at their problems from a different angle and give them the strength to try.

Tamar Chansky, the author of *Freeing Your Child from Negative Thinking* (2008), writes in his book that negative thinking is a close relative of anxiety. A negative mindset makes us think of the worst that could happen and ultimately demotivate us. Anxiety does the same. It tricks the mind into thinking that failure is imminent, and therefore, it kills the will to even try. Such thoughts control our actions, and it is common sense that persistent, negative thoughts can never yield positive outcomes.

Thus, negative thoughts must be countered with positive and productive thoughts that promise better results. As easy as it is to say, thinking positively doesn't happen overnight. It isn't a switch you can turn off and on whenever you feel like it. There is a cognitive pattern involved that can take months to adjust to. Before we learn about how we can put cognitive reframing to the test, what benefits it can yield, and how to help children reframe their negative thoughts and emotions, there are some cognitive distortions that are common in everyone. Their identification is necessary if you want to know what exactly you are working with.

These cognitive distortions are the reasons why children, as well as adults, have a difficult time looking at the bright side of things.

- **All-or-Nothing Thinking:** It involves looking at things in only two categories (good or bad, black or white, etc.). Children who have such a mentality have a hard time seeing the shades of gray or reading things between the lines. They think they can fail or succeed; win or lose; and have or not have things.

- **Emotional Reasoning:** Here, a child feels that if they feel something, it must be true. They believe what they feel without any evidence. Their feelings dominate their critical thinking skills.

- **Mind Reading:** Children think that they know and understand what others are thinking about them and feel like they aren't good enough.

- **Catastrophizing:** Here, a child magnifies a problem and blows it out of proportion.

- **Discounting the Positive:** In this type of cognitive distortion, a child minimizes a good thing intentionally. Even when they succeed, they don't feel joy or happiness because they think it is a one-time thing or generally not a big deal.

- **Mental Filter:** Here, a child discounts all the positive and neutral aspects of an experience and only focuses on the negative. It's like they ponder over the one bad compliment they received from someone over the nine other positive compliments they received.

- **Personalization:** As the name suggests, here, what a child feels creates everything about themselves even when it isn't. They blame themselves for things out of their control and take everything personally.

- **Overgeneralization:** A child feels like one small setback or failure determines their true worth. They assume that if they fail at something once, it will become a universal pattern.

- **Labeling:** In labeling, children are quick to label themselves and others and can never see past that label. Once they have made up their mind about someone, there is little wiggle room left to change their thinking.

- **Fortune-Telling:** Here, a child keeps making scenarios about their future in a negative way. Their thoughts affect their actions and ultimately result in failure or loss.

How Reframing Works and Helps

The process of reframing negative thoughts into positive ones encompasses changing, discarding, and modifying a negative thought pattern. Like the frame and a picture are two different things, reframing looks at a given situation in two different lights. You can apply the same concept to any given situation you or your child faces and help them see the good that comes from it. Even our mistakes have something to teach us. Our failures and losses serve as lessons to change and modify our actions and behaviors.

In reframing, we begin by labeling the negative emotions and separate them from the situation we are in. It is like cause and effect—we determine what led to an outburst or a temper tantrum. Was it a situation that triggered the emotion or vice versa? Then, we prioritize what's more important. We form a frame of reference to organize and distinguish between positive and negative behavior.

For example, if a teenager is acting demotivated about a breakup, you can help them see the good side of it.

Perhaps their partner was toxic. Perhaps their partner didn't allow your kid to be themselves. Perhaps there was poor chemistry between them. Since the breakup is an event, now it is on them how they are going to process it. Are they going to stay depressed about it or be happy about the independence and freedom they have? Helping them see things in such a manner where they can distinguish between two different behaviors and emotions and then reframe their own negative thinking is what reframing is all about. As a parent, you remind them of all the things they have gained from something as opposed to remaining focused on all that they have lost. It's like telling a child that they are possessive about their toys as opposed to saying that they are selfish or hate to share their toys with others.

Cognitive reframing turns negative thoughts and experiences into opportunities for growth and change. It helps change a child's viewpoint of seeing things. They stop seeing a problem as a trial and view it as a challenge they are willing to try their luck at. It encourages them to think of all the possible conclusions that can happen if they try.

Cognitive reframing also validates their emotions. Throughout the process, you don't try to disregard or ignore how they are feeling. Instead, you help them make sense of those emotions by understanding the cause and effect. You make them realize that what they are feeling is a natural reaction they shouldn't ignore or run away from. You teach them to label it and embrace it. However, at the same time, you tell them how their negative feelings are often overimaginative and overgeneralized.

Finally, cognitive reframing promotes self-compassion. We are often harsh when it comes to ourselves and kinder when speaking about someone else. You can help your child make sense of a situation by asking them what they should suggest to their friend if they were in the same situation. You can make them realize that we are often kinder to others than we are to ourselves.

Overcoming Negative Thoughts Using Reframing

Like adults, children are prone to negative thinking. They can make them feel insecure about themselves, cause meltdowns, promote confusion, and become the reason for fights. Since negative thoughts encourage negative actions, teaching young children to counter them is important. However, the concept can be a little abstract for them. As soon as you have identified a bad thought, it is time to change. Below are some practical approaches that can help you get started:

Write Everything Down

If a child fails an exam and thinks that they will forever remain a failure, here's how you are going to help them reframe their thinking. You ask them to write down the emotions that arose when they first heard about their grade. Write it in one column of a page. In the second column, write about something positive that they gained from the experience. For example, they can feel good about the fact that they studied so hard for it and learned about many new things. That thought, as opposed to the first one, seems more encouraging and promising.

You can also role-play a negative event and challenge your child to find the silver lining in it. If they succeed, reward them. If not, then help them see it and discuss the benefits.

Rephrase

Write down a list of negative emotions or actions, and ask your child to reframe them into something positive. They can change the sentence structure, wording, or come up with a completely new sentence on their own. For example, if the sentence sounds something like this: "No one wants to play with me," it can be rephrased into something like this: "I can name three people who want to play with me."

Make A "Strengths" List

Finally, help them identify their strengths. Ask them to generate a list of all the good qualities, skills, and talents they see in them. If they can't come up with many, ask other members of the family or their friends to come with some. Sometimes, children are quick to overlook certain characteristics like selflessness, patience, kindness, humility, etc. Hearing others compliment them will boost their morale and confidence.

Chapter 4:

Create a Positive Environment to Grow Up In

To foster a positive mentality, children need a positive environment to grow in. You can't expect a child to grow up with a positive mindset when they see their parents fighting constantly or having arguments over small things. Not only does it distort their perception of healthy relationships but it also makes for a negative environment. There is little consideration and respect shown toward one another. Giving them a happy and positive environment is, therefore, a necessity for their healthy mental and emotional growth. You must surround them with love and consideration. They should feel loved, validated, and treasured in the house. They should be able to mingle around freely and be open and communicative. They should have friends and neighbors who often visit and add to their state of happiness. As a parent, you must know that it is important for building healthy social skills, too.

How can you provide them with a space where they feel loved, protected, and guided? How can you assure them of the love that you have for them and teach them to be kind to themselves, too? How can you help them counter negative thoughts using self-compassion techniques and activities to instill their faith in their abilities and skills?

In this chapter, we will be talking about it and see how being just their parent isn't enough.

Be Affectionate and Friendly

Secrecy, possessiveness, and the need for personal space become basic needs as children grow. However, this shouldn't prevent parents from playing an active role in their child's life. As children, they shouldn't feel the need to keep secrets from you or demand some space. In an ideal household, they should come to you to talk about anything and everything including, love, friendships, and sexual relationships. How much they disclose can differ, but as parents, you have a right to know if they are being safe about the choices they have, hanging out with the right group of people, and if they are engaging in healthy behaviors or not. That being said, how you interact with them says a lot about how willing your children are to share things with you.

Often parents don't realize that their reactions and know-it-all attitude are what drives away children. If they feel unappreciated, neglected, or ignored, they are likely to take their matters elsewhere. Therefore, the first thing you need is to try to be their friend. Ask about what's going on in their lives, show interest in the things they do or the people they hang out with, befriend their friends, and invite them to come over frequently so that you know what they are up to.

Also, schedule free time to just have a chat with them or watch a movie or show together. This will make for some great bonding time; once you are done, you can discuss the plot, character, and ending. The goal is to make them feel important and valued by being affectionate.

Lend them an ear when you find them demotivated or sad about something. Validate their feelings and be kind and empathetic. They don't always need advice, rather, they just someone to vent their feelings to.

Be expressive with how you feel about them. Remind them how grateful and appreciative you are to have them in your life. Compliment them when they do something remotely positive, so they can repeat that behavior the next time. Talk positively about their talents and skills in front of others so that their confidence levels increase. Make time for hugs, kisses, and pats on the back.

Help Overcome Fears

Negative thoughts and emotions often come wrapped with fears. The fear of failure, the fear of missing out, or the fear of being ridiculed are all types of genuine concerns that can take up space in a child's mind. Every child succumbs to one or more of these and gets left behind. With some assistance and attention from you, they can overcome these using the right strategies and approaches. Many people suggest exposure therapy where you expose the person to what they are afraid of. However, in a child's case, this isn't always the best approach. Unlike others, they may not comprehend the wisdom behind the approach and become more scared. What you can do instead is the following:

- **Be There:** Whenever they need help, guidance, or comfort, be present. Your attention and interest in how they feel and experience are enough to show your love and affection to them. When they know that they have someone backing them up and supporting them, they won't feel lonely or think that they have to overcome their fears alone.

- **Have Patience:** They aren't going to get over something that scares the life out of them overnight. You have to keep being patient and gradually make things easier for them. For many parents, it can become frustrating when the child asks to check under the bed for monsters several hours in the night. However, disregarding their fears will suggest that you don't care enough. Revealing your negative emotions can upset them and increase their nervousness about what they fear.

- **Empathize:** Acknowledge and help them label their fears. Then, ask to embrace them and see what happens. For example, in the case of monsters under the bed, encourage them to be confident enough to look for the monsters themselves or suggest alternatives like keeping the lights open, saying a prayer before bed, or reading stories involving people overcoming their fears.

- **Make Plans to Conquer Fears, but Take Things Slow:** For example, if they are afraid of the water, try suggesting going to the beach for collecting seashells and not for bathing. Then, gradually encourage them to dip their feet into the water. If they are afraid of heights, suggest building a treehouse together. Ideally, the construction will involve ladders and gathering branches and tools. Slowly encourage them to climb the tree by climbing the ladder first. Likewise, if they are afraid of fires, plan a camping trip that involves toasting marshmallows over an open fire and telling interesting stories. The more fun they have, the less worried they will be about their fear.

- **When Making Such Plans, Ask Them to Help Devise Them:** The more involved they are with how they want to overcome their fear, the more motivated they will be. Take their suggestions into account and compliment on how brave they are to even try. For instance, if your child is fearful of you leaving their room and working in another room, ask them how you can make them feel better. They can come up with suggestions like permission to check up on you every five minutes. Putting this to practice, you can increase the amount of time between check-ins over time and teach them how to stay in their room without supervision.

Become Their Biggest Motivator

Even as adults, we experience nervousness and anxiety. Getting into a room full of strangers; fear of missing the bus; worrying about not having enough savings at the end of the month; or stressing about your child or partner's health are all fears that make us anxious. Despite knowing that everything will eventually be okay, we lose confidence in ourselves. This leads to poor concentration and poor performance which messes things up.

Our kids can experience the same. With all the negativity surrounding them, it can be hard to remain spirited and optimistic. What they need is someone that would cheer them on, support them, love them unconditionally, and be available. They need encouragement: Maybe give them a little hug or a pat on the back when they do something good. They need to know that there is someone they can trust and rely on. That motivator has to be the parent—you!

As parents, we need to be more appreciative and motivating so that we can raise individuals that are proud of themselves and self-reliant. We need to raise individuals that don't seek validation from others and are confident of who they are. This is possible only when they say, "I can," instead of, "I can't."

Being their guide and showing appreciation and motivation from your end can work wonders in boosting their self-esteem and confidence. It can make them feel more in control of their lives and become independent. If they think they aren't physically attractive, teach them how to overcome their lack of confidence by commenting on their best features.

You can also encourage them by helping them set goals. Take out some time apart and talk to them about their interests. See where their passions lie. Then, create a list of their short-term and long-term goals. Assist them in breaking down those goals into smaller goals and set deadlines. Provide them with the tools, resources, and guidance they need to achieve them. Track their progress every week and celebrate their wins.

Keep them excited about the goals they have set. Show excitement for them, too. The positivity and adrenaline about the goals inside the house will fuel positivity in the surroundings. They will feel more appreciated and loved when they see that everyone's on board with them and cheering them on.

Show affection and compliment them over small wins and successes. Celebrate good grades and include them in important decisions like what they need from the grocery store, where they would like to eat out over the weekend, or what chores they would like to pick. Doing so will make them feel like an important part of the house and make them feel validated.

Chapter 5:

Teach About Loving and

Sharing

Positive actions and habits yield positive results. When we encourage children to be positive, we don't only tell them to think positively. We tell them to form their habits and actions around those feelings and emotions. Yet how can this be nurtured?

We have all seen videos of children being ungrateful for their Christmas presents. We see them throwing tantrums because Santa didn't get them what they asked for. Yes, it can be frustrating, but it's part of life. The reason this happens is that those children lack the skills to appreciate and acknowledge what they have. Their parents have spoon-fed them their whole lives; they feel privileged. However, take the same gift to someone at an orphanage, and you will see how grateful and appreciative those children are for the same gifts your child rejected.

The reason: They don't know the value of things, the emotions behind the gift, and the money that was spent getting it. They think they deserve much better. This also suggests that your child is unappreciative of the many facilities they get without asking, like food, shelter, clothes, and the Internet.

However, showing gratitude for things that others take for granted is another positive trait to cultivate. Children who are appreciative of the things in their lives are also careful about using them. They may not have paid for it from their pocket money, but they know the value of it and the sentiment behind this.

When children are unappreciative, they are also selfish. They don't like to share their things with others and like to remain in control. For example, if they get a new PlayStation, they may invite their friends over but only let them watch. This type of mentality also breeds a negative mindset. In this type of thinking, the child feels that if they share, others will damage their goods. If they never share, how can they learn of the joy that comes from sharing? Therefore, in this chapter, we will look at how developing a positive mindset will make children become more grateful and become better companions to their friends.

How Helping Others Inspires Positivity

The act of lending a hand to someone in need says a lot about a person. Not many have the time or resources to help others. However, those who don't miss out on the joy that comes from it. Assisting others enhances feelings of positivity. Take volunteering, for instance. It is a selfless act that doesn't involve the usual give and take. There are no expectations—just happiness that is received by both parties. Individuals that engage in acts such as volunteering, mentoring, and counseling others without anything in return have higher self-esteem. They have better overall well-being. They lead meaningful and purposeful lives.

According to Dr. Sonja Lyubomirsky, people who go out of their way to help others and offer aid out of kindness are happier over time (Lyubomirsky et al., 2005). If this is true, imagine the benefits it can have for your child! When children develop compassion for others, respect each other's opinions and viewpoints. Be considerate toward them, as it makes them feel good about themselves. When they experience the joy firsthand that comes from helping others, it makes them more optimistic about life.

Helping others has also been linked to cultivating a sense of inner peace, belongingness, and gratitude. When children experience the joy that comes from sharing their time and resources with those less privileged than them, it gives them a sense of fulfillment. It's an emotion that can only be felt when we are kind to one another. For example, a child can assist an elderly person in setting up their outfit, reminding them to take medication, taking them on small walks, and helping them with day-to-day chores. Doing all these things will make them feel grateful toward their body for all the work that it does. Spending time with them will also enrich their being with some amazing life stories and lessons for the future.

Volunteering also instills a positive attitude. The act of giving leaves people feeling satisfied. Their system is filled with a sense of accomplishment like they have done something worthy. Such emotions increase positivity on a chemical level. Helping others leads to an increase of dopamine, the "feel-good" hormone, in the brain that adds to our happiness.

To many, helping others gives them a purpose. From setting up charitable galas and fundraisers to organizing games and toys for young children, some people spend their whole lives devoted to the act of giving. It gives their life an entirely new meaning. Engaging children in such activities from an early age will help them feel good about themselves and add meaning to their lives. Whatever their age or situation, you can be sure that helping others will make them feel better and take their mind away from the worries they carry.

Looking at this link between positivity, meaningfulness, and helping others, it can be assumed that over time, teaching children about loving and sharing promotes better mental health. This is an essential need for today, as many youngsters struggle with finding something worth doing in their lives. Activities such as helping others allow them to engage in social interactions, make friends, and create a support system based on shared interests. All these facts promote better mental and emotional health.

Activities That Promote Loving and Sharing

Young children can help their parents around the house, take care of their siblings, and assist with weekly tasks like getting the clothes ready, washing the car, or helping with the groceries. Doing so will not only instill responsibility but also develop the habit of organization and management. House management and organization are important life skills that every school-age child must learn.

To promote the act of loving and sharing, below are some great and fun ideas to foster a positive mindset in children.

Happiness Treasure Hunt

Start with creating a list of tasks your child has to perform. For instance, if you plan to take them to the park, the list of positive actions can involve the following:

- High-five three children.

- Say hello to five kids.

- Compliment a friend.

- Share your snacks with two friends.

- Give someone a gift on the way.

Encourage your child to finish off as many tasks as they can from the list. Set a reward for them at the end. Also, ask how the exercise made them feel when they finish. If they feel happier, make it a weekly thing. You can also substitute the tasks depending on where you are going. For example, you can create separate lists when going to a community event, welfare center, charitable organization, or the beach.

Create a Positivity Jar

Take an empty jar and ask your children to write one positive thing that happened to them every day and to put it in the jar. Once a week, sit down together and give those paper slips a read. You and your spouse should also join in and put something positive that happened in the positivity jar. This is a great exercise to remind your children of all the good that has happened to them in the past week. Every time you notice them being sad, you can ask them to take out a strip of paper and read it. It will instantly take them back to that date and event and make them happier.

You can also create a gratitude jar in a similar way. As opposed to writing about one positive thing, you can write about one thing that you are grateful for every day and put it in the jar. You can create a separate jar for your child and request them to do the same. Then, review the things over the weekend or after a month. They will learn to be thankful for all that they have.

Happiness Journal

Encourage children to keep journals tracking their happiest moments like going on a dream trip, eating at their favorite diner, having a sleepover at a friend's house, getting good grades, or performing at a school event. When they write down their emotions and how they felt in those moments of joy, they become a permanent memory. They can always go back and read about those memories and relive those moments in their minds. They can also record their disappointments in life so that they can reflect on the things they did wrong and how they can improve on them. Journaling is a great practice, as it becomes an outlet for emotional worries and sharing of happy moments. Reading about their happiest milestones can set a positive vibe and motivate them when they feel like giving up.

Chapter 6:

Encourage Development of Skills and Talent

Some parents are quick to thwart their child's creative side because it doesn't conform to the ideals or practices they are trying to teach or model. They want their children to focus solely on their academics without giving any heed to the many amazing skills and talents that enable them to feel confident and nurture valuable, lifelong habits. For instance, a stamp collection might not seem like a lucrative hobby for them to enjoy, but there is a lot they can learn from collecting stamps. It can teach them about the history of those stamps; where they originated; how they became popular; names of countries they belong to; people or places on them; the organization; and the value of money. They can improve their geographical awareness and actively enhance their counting and categorizing skills. That is just one of the many activities and hobbies. There can be many others which, if nurtured with the right intention and interest, can contribute toward the development of some essential life skills.

Having said that, parents must also encourage young children to follow their passions and invest in them. If they want to see the world, encourage them to learn a new language. If they love to watch Animal Planet, have them watch child-friendly documentaries to know more about the animals they love to watch.

If they seem interested in activities like painting, singing, or playing an instrument, help them nourish those skills by providing the right tools and resources. Doing so will not only make them master those skills but also improve their confidence. It will encourage their creative side, and they will feel more driven to be better. As parents, we should all celebrate originality— no matter how unprofessional it may seem. Doing so will eventually make them think positively about themselves and develop a positive mindset.

Encouraging children to try new things and activities begins with recognizing where their strengths and interests lie. Are they more drawn toward history and stories about famous figures? Are they into music or any particular form of it? Are they interested in knowing about the stars and how they revolve around the sun? Do scientific experiments excite them?

Their interests reveal a lot about the kind of individual they are. Harness those and increase the time spent on those interests. Then, if their interests persist or grow, provide them with the tools and materials required to excel in that art form. For instance, if they are into classical music and particularly interested in playing violin, enroll them in a short course so that they can master the basics during the summer break. Similarly, if they are interested in drawing or animation, let them take a diploma course in it to learn how to use different types of software.

Recognize where their strengths lie and help them develop those skills to nurture those talents. As they learn more about the hobby and become good at it, getting compliments from everyone for it will ultimately lead to a positive mindset and confidence boost. They will see that doing good at anything earns respect, affection, and appreciation. They will learn how investing time to improve yields more success. They will learn to overcome obstacles as they will recall their progress from day one and how far they have come from there.

How Positive Thinking and Developing Skill Sets Are Connected

Research into positive thinking and the development of skills reveals that positive thinking offers more than just an upbeat attitude toward life. In fact, it helps young children see that their potential is unlimited, and the possibilities are endless. It promotes hope and promises betterment. It tells them that they can grow and master anything they wish to learn about or take on. Having a positive attitude aids them to find real value in life by building essential life skills that come in handy as they grow older.

The impact of positive thinking and the development of skills is studied in great depth by Barbara Fredrickson, a psychology researcher at the University of North Carolina. She has many publications offering insightful evidence into the world of positive thinking. In one of these landmark papers, she elaborately discussed how positive thinking and the development of essential life skills are interconnected. According to Fredrickson (2004), the benefits of thinking positively and developing important life skills don't stop after a few minutes of happiness.

Using a real-world example, she tries to explain the connection between the two. Imagine a child running outside, playing in the mud, swinging on branches, making new friends, and working together. All these actions may look naive, but the habits that are drawn from these are remarkable. Being physically active can land them a scholarship due to their athleticism. Making friends can help them avoid becoming socially awkward and form healthy relationships with everyone. Working as a team can help them learn how to cooperate and work with others using healthy boundaries. They also learn skills such as effective communication, active listening, empathy, kindness, and many other social skills that will eventually help them once they enter adulthood (Fredrickson, 2004).

Encouraging Positive Action

You can prompt positive action by encouraging them to seek out new skills and activities. If they are eager to explore, curious about the things they don't know, and show an interest in active learning, then use some of the tips below to get started.

Show Support

Some children are slow learners. They take longer to pick up on basic concepts or follow instructions and guidelines very carefully. However, this shouldn't mean that you discourage them and request them to try something else. Show support of how far they have come—even if it is just the beginning. The idea is to encourage the continuation of learning at whatever pace they feel comfortable with. Showing frustration or taking control from them will only discourage further action and make a child feel incompetent. Therefore, always make it a point to celebrate small wins like learning to play "Happy Birthday" on the piano or hitting the ball into the net when playing soccer. Motivating them, cheering them for their wins, and being there to support them is important for their positive growth.

Emphasize Shared Experiences

Be interested in finding new topics to talk about or things to do. For example, you two can watch a movie together and then discuss the roles of the protagonist. You can even sign up for a dance or cooking class together and have a fun-filled day at knocking your heels or baking the best chocolate cake in the world. You can also start house renovation projects together like setting up IKEA furniture or building a new house for your pet. Here, the goal is to connect with your little one and promote taking positive actions by helping them find new things to enjoy. With you by their side, they will feel more confident.

Practice Positive Affirmations

Positive affirmations are words or phrases that you repeat like a mantra to yourself. It encourages positive action as well as trying new challenges. Repeating positive affirmations daily helps you feel confident. Positive affirmations are usually in the present tense, meaning what you say or think about is something you are capable of doing. This tricks the mind into thinking so and helps in promoting positive action. For example, telling yourself, "I am enough" is a great way to initiate positive action. It may just be three words, but it can mean anything you have in mind. For example, if you feel unworthy, repeating this will restore your self-worth. Repeating this when you feel scared can make you feel in control and alleviate the anxiety you feel. Repeating the mantra when you are trying something risky can make it seem easier.

Now, imagine your child repeating more of these motivational affirmations to themselves every day. Imagine the impact it can have on their self-esteem, self-worth, and confidence in their abilities. They will feel energized to try anything they set their mind to.

Chapter 7:

Nurture a Growth Mindset

Every child needs to believe in something with every cell in their body. Only when they believe in it so much can they thrive. Their belief system is shaped by what they see. Be aware: they can be quite observant when it comes to imitating your actions and ideas.

In general, children either have a fixed or growth mindset. According to a fixed mindset, intelligence is a gifted ability that one can only have from when they are born. A growth mindset, in contrast, believes that intelligence and wisdom can increase if one tries. Children with a fixed mindset believe they are born with a certain personality; have a fixed amount of good and bad habits; have limited potential, creativity, and intelligence; and that there is simply nothing they can do about it.

Children with a growth mindset, however, think differently. They believe that there is always extra room for improvement and growth. They believe that they can develop the skills they lack; gain more knowledge and wisdom; and change themselves to become a better version of themselves. They don't believe that there are limitations to their growth and development. Children with a growth mindset don't stop at anything, are eager to challenge and take risks, and discover new things. They are passionate about exploration and getting more acquainted with the things they don't know about.

Children with a fixed mindset often come up with excuses when asked to try new things. They seem reluctant, afraid, and anxious. Their brain tells them that they will fail. This starts a chain of negative thinking and ends with failure. Since the results are what they predicted, it further reinforces their belief in the fact that they were right all along.

On the other hand, if we, as parents, nurture a growth mindset, we can show them that the fear of failure can be overcome if they give it a try. We can tell them that to overcome any fear or limitations, one has to try new things or think creatively to come up with more promising solutions. Despite all that, if they still fail, we can remind them that failure doesn't mean that they are unintelligent or incompetent. It just shows that they need to work on growing some more and expand their potential. As soon as they start to see their mistakes and failures as lessons they can learn from, they will be on the way to greatness.

Since these two mindsets begin to manifest at an early age, their capacity for happiness and optimism is also developed around the same time. Therefore, if you wish to nurture a more positive outlook toward life, you need to introduce them to new things, encourage taking on challenges, and offer to console them when they fail.

What parents do instead is two things: criticize and restrict them. They criticize children for poor performance, further damaging their confidence. They restrict them from exploring new things, labeling them as wasteful or useless. They limit their potential without even knowing, and when they fail, all thanks to a lack of knowledge, the parents further blame them. This becomes a vicious cycle in which the child feels trapped and unable to grow.

The Benefits of Nurturing a Growth Mindset

There are several benefits to developing a growth mindset. As per several studies, a growth mindset is linked with better test results in exams, improved eagerness to discover the undiscovered, better problem-solving skills, and a strong desire toward the love of learning. Children with a fixed mindset are afraid to leave the nest. They like to stay in their haven and miss out on opportunities that are in front of them. They think that trying something new and then failing at it would make them appear dumb in front of others. They fear being ridiculed and stick to what they know. Although this isn't a bad approach, it just prevents them from going out and doing something they might be great at. For instance, a child may be a natural at pitching a ball, but how would they know if they never step outside the house or hold a ball?

Over time, such individuals grow up to lead monotonous lives and waste their life in tedious jobs. They also miss out on enjoying the process of learning something new and gradually becoming an expert at it. Instead, they are more concerned with exhibiting what they already know.

Children with a growth mindset challenge things. They don't sit back and accept fate as it is. They try and keep trying harder the next time. They don't settle for things—they thrive for them. Children who fuel their curiosity are more confident. They know that to get more knowledge, it would require them to seek out more information which can only come from books, experiences, and people. This means that they tend to be more communicative and social. They enjoy the process of learning and hone their problem-solving skills.

As stated before, a growth mindset improves your child's test results. Carol Dweck's study on children's fixed versus growth mindset followed the participant's lives throughout secondary school. She found that children who had a growth mindset landed in high-paying jobs, were happier in their relationships, and had better academic performance than those with a fixed mindset (Dweck, 2019). She also found that children with a growth mindset had creative and prospering careers as opposed to those with a fixed mindset. It was solely because children with a growth mindset were positive about their options. They were quicker to grab opportunities to succeed and excel in their careers and lives.

A growth mindset also sets children up for life. Did you know Albert Einstein wasn't always a bright student? His teachers believed that he would remain a slow learner all his life and never achieve anything remotely great. What happened next shocked the entire world and continues to shock many scientists. He could have given up and believed what his teachers told him; instead, he overcame his struggles and challenged his brain. He put in the work, and year after year, his knowledge grew. Einstein, like others, viewed learning as a positive and necessary action.

How to Stimulate a Growth Mindset

Mindsets are important at determining more than just your child's success or happiness. It also impacts their mental and emotional health. If they feel that they are incompetent and bad at things, it can lead to stress and anxiety. They will feel anxious around those who are honest and ready to take on challenges. Their efforts won't yield the results and experiences they hope for. As a parent, we can change that and influence the kind of mindset they breed. We can teach them how to master things and take risks. We can teach them how to problem solve and think creatively. We can teach them to look at the bright side of things even when they feel like they have failed or lost.

A growth mindset supercharges a child's ability to grow and learn. Parents and educators play a crucial role in what the child learns, how they think, and how they approach uncertainty. Together, we have the power to steer them in the right direction that leads to a promising and positive mindset.

Below are three ideas to begin teaching children how to develop a growth mindset:

The Power of Yet

The power of yet is an interesting activity. A lot of times, when you ask children to do something, they come up with excuses such as, "I don't know how to do that," I can't do that," "I'm not good at it," etc. All these are thoughts prompted by the inner critic. It's like having a voice constantly telling you what to do and not do. Even if the child feels confident, the inner critic reminds them of a past negative experience, stopping them from trying again. This type of negative self-talk can be damaging to developing a positive mindset. Here's what you are going to do. Every time your child comes up with an excuse to not try something because they feel they won't be good at it, tell them that they aren't good at it "yet," but they eventually will be if they try.

For example, if you ask your child to fold the laundry and they say that they don't know how to, tell them that they don't know how to do it yet. Then, proceed to show them how to do it and ask them to mimic your actions. Repeat it a few times until they get a proper grasp of it and can do it themselves. Apply the same technique to everything they struggle with or feel afraid to try.

Bravery Ladders

The second exercise comes from Dr. Donna B. Pincus who explains the concept well in her book, *Growing Up Brave*, for children who suffer from fear and anxiety (Pincus, 2012). The idea behind a bravery ladder is simple. It begins with the drawing of a ladder on a sheet of paper. Then, on the top of the ladder, you ask your child to write about the fear or anxiety they have. An example of it can be stage fright or making friends.

Next, on each step of the ladder, ask the child to come up with ideas and solutions to help them overcome that anxiety. For example, in case of stage fright, they can begin by rehearsing lines from a play in front of the mirror. This could be the first step. From there on, they then move toward the second step that can involve demonstrating their role in front of you or their friends. The third step can involve signing up for a play at school and so on. They can gradually increase the size of their audience and then ultimately overcome their fear by performing in the play.

Conclusion

The cultivation of a positive mindset fosters resilience, independence, and confidence in children—both young and adults. It prepares them to handle life's difficult situations with their critical thinking and optimistic take on things. Even if they fail, a positive mindset prevents them from breaking down or viewing themselves as a failure. Every failure or setback becomes a learning opportunity, every mistake another chance to improve, and every criticism becomes a source of inspiration to do better the next time. With positive thinking come positive actions. Positive actions yield positive habits. These positive habits result in the development of healthy social, emotional, and important life skills such as compassion, kindness, humility, discipline, and self-reliance. Children who are raised to have a positive mindset are more successful than those whose minds are filled with negative feelings about themselves and others. They are quick to give up and surrender. They fixate on their mistakes and think that there is no room for improvement.

That being said, parents have a crucial role in the development of a positive mindset. Children that are brought up in homes where they feel loved, appreciated, secure, and valued develop a positive mindset. Children who are encouraged to explore their passions, try new things, and take risks with the support of their parents excel and accomplish great things. When children know the value of love and sharing, they become accountable for their actions, words, and behaviors. They treat others with respect and kindness. When children are given the right tools to overcome their fears and resolve problems, they develop a growth mindset and believe that anything is possible.

When parents teach them to reframe their negative thinking with positive experiences and ideas, they build resilience. They can see the silver lining in things and view the glass as half full. Their perspective about life changes for the better.

However, all of this is only possible when you, as a parent, model the same behaviors and practices that you are trying to preach. It all comes down to how you live your life, deal with everyday stresses, and overcome your problems. If they see you struggling, arguing, or being pessimistic about life, they are going to do the same. If they see you ignoring their needs, disrespecting others, or not showing consideration toward others, they are going to learn the same. If they notice you getting disheartened and giving up after a setback, they are going to follow in your footsteps, too.

Therefore, be wise and wary of how you present yourself to them. Your actions, gestures, body language, and behaviors should emit positivity. If it does, your child shouldn't have any problem picking up those habits either.

Thank you for giving this book a read. I hope you loved reading it as much as I enjoyed writing it. It would make me the happiest person on earth if you would take a moment to leave an honest review. All you have to do is visit the site where you purchased this book: It's that simple! The review doesn't have to be a full-fledged paragraph; a few words will do. Your few words will help others decide if this is what they should be reading as well. Thank you in advance, and best of luck with your parenting adventures. Every moment is a joyous one with a child.

References

10 ways to be a role model to your children. (2011, September 14). All pro Dad. https://www.allprodad.com/10-ways-to-be-a-role-model-to-your-children/

10 ways to encourage positive thinking in your child. (n.d.). Indiaparenting.com. https://www.indiaparenting.com/10-ways-to-encourage-positive-thinking-in-your-child.html

Asher, L. (2020, September 15). *What role do parents play in developing a "growth mindset" in children?* India Today. https://www.indiatoday.in/education-today/featurephilia/story/what-role-do-parents-play-in-developing-a-growth-mindset-in-children-1722033-2020-09-15

Auer, D. (2019, May 2). *Health benefits of volunteering.* Thriveglobal.com.

https://thriveglobal.com/stories/health-benefits-of-volunteering/

Bamford, C., & Lagattuta, K. H. (2011). Looking on the bright side: Children's knowledge about the benefits of positive versus negative thinking. *Child Development*, *83*(2), no-no. https://doi.org/10.1111/j.1467-8624.2011.01706.x

Chen, L., Bae, S. R., Battista, C., Qin, S., Chen, T., Evans, T. M., & Menon, V. (2018). Positive attitude toward math supports early academic success: Behavioral evidence and neurocognitive mechanisms. *Psychological Science*, *29*(3), 390–402. https://doi.org/10.1177/0956797617735528

Clear, J. (2019, April 22). *How positive thinking builds your skills, boosts your health, and improves your work*. James Clear. https://jamesclear.com/positive-thinking

Cullins, A. (2017a). *7 activities to help your child develop a positive attitude*. Big Life Journal. https://biglifejournal.com/blogs/blog/children-positive-attitude

Cullins, A. (2017b, August 27). *7 ways to encourage your child to try new things*. Big Life Journal. https://biglifejournal.com/blogs/blog/encourage-child-to-try-new-things

Driscoll, L. (2019, January 15). *Helping children challenge negative thinking*. Social Emotional Workshop. https://www.socialemotionalworkshop.com/challenge-negative-thinking/

Dweck, C. S. (2019). The choice to make a difference. *Perspectives on Psychological Science, 14*(1), 21–25. https://doi.org/10.1177/1745691618804180

Entin, E. (2012, January 19). *The power of positive thinking*. The Atlantic. https://www.theatlantic.com/health/archive/2012/01/the-power-of-positive-thinking/251500/

Fredrickson, B. L. (2004). The broaden–and–build theory of positive emotions. *Philosophical Transactions of the Royal Society of London. Series B: Biological Sciences, 359*(1449), 1367–1377. https://doi.org/10.1098/rstb.2004.1512

Garey, J. (n.d.). *How to change negative thinking patterns.* Child Mind Institute. https://childmind.org/article/how-to-change-negative-thinking-patterns/

Ghandour, R. M., Sherman, L. J., Vladutiu, C. J., Ali, M. M., Lynch, S. E., Bitsko, R. H., & Blumberg, S. J. (2019). Prevalence and treatment of depression, anxiety, and conduct problems in US children. *The Journal of Pediatrics, 206*, 256-267.e3. https://doi.org/10.1016/j.jpeds.2018.09.021

Grunbaum, J. A., Kann, L., Kinchen, S. A., Ross, J. G., Gowda, V. R., Collins, J. L., & Kolbe, L. J. (2000). Youth risk behavior surveillance national alternative high school youth risk behavior survey, united states, 1998. *Journal of*

School Health, *70*(1), 5–17.
https://doi.org/10.1111/j.1746-
1561.2000.tb06439.x

Howe, C. (2018, June 22). *Qualities of A good role model.*
Seedling Mentors.
https://seedlingmentors.org/qualities-of-a-
good-role-model/

Importance of a positive attitude for students. (2019, February
27). Your Therapy Source.
https://www.yourtherapysource.com/blog1/20
19/02/26/the-benefits-of-positive-attitudes-in-
students/

Johnston, L. D., O'Malley, P. M., & Bachman, J. G.
(2003). Monitoring the future: National results
on adolescent drug use: Overview of key
findings. *FOCUS*, *1*(2), 213–234.
https://doi.org/10.1176/foc.1.2.213

Lyubomirsky, S., King, L., & Diener, E. (2005). The
benefits of frequent positive affect: Does
happiness lead to success? *Psychological Bulletin*,

131(6), 803–855.

https://doi.org/10.1037/0033-2909.131.6.803

Mathew, A. A. (2018, April 25). *The power of positive thinking: 8 tips for children, the power of positivity.* Www.parentcircle.com. https://www.parentcircle.com/tips-for-power-of-positive-thinking-in-children/article

Molina, K. (2017, December 13). *10 ways to help your children develop a positive attitude.* Medium. https://medium.com/@kaytmolina/10-ways-to-help-your-children-develop-a-positive-attitude-e74611c71fad

Morin, A. (2019). *How cognitive reframing is used in mental health.* Verywell Mind. https://www.verywellmind.com/reframing-defined-2610419

Patton, G. C., Tollit, M. M., Romaniuk, H., Spence, S. H., Sheffield, J., & Sawyer, M. G. (2011). A prospective study of the effects of optimism on adolescent health risks. *PEDIATRICS*, *127*(2),

308–316. https://doi.org/10.1542/peds.2010-0748

Positive thinking: How to foster in your child. (2012, July 25). Www.aboutkidshealth.ca. https://www.aboutkidshealth.ca/Article?contentid=629&language=English#/

Pincus, D. (2012). Growing up brave : Expert strategies for helping your child overcome fear, stress, and anxiety. Little, Brown and Co.

Power of positivity. (2019, July 18). Early Learning Childhood Education. https://musicearlychildhoodpresenter.com/power-of-positivity/

Prasanna, S. (n.d.). *Power of positivity: Imparting the power of positive thinking to your kids – tutorix blog.* Tutorix. Retrieved August 19, 2021, from https://www.tutorix.com/blog/power-of-positivity-imparting-the-power-of-positive-thinking-to-your-kids/

Raina, K. (2019, January 4). *10 effective ways to be a positive role model for your kids*. Parenting.firstcry.com. https://parenting.firstcry.com/articles/parents-as-a-role-model-shape-your-childs-life-in-a-positive-way/

Reframing negative thinking patterns. (2021, February 22). The Light Program. https://thelightprogram.pyramidhealthcarepa.com/gaining-perspective-reframing-negative-thinking-patterns/

Rudy, M. (2019). *9 ways to reframe negative thoughts into positive affirmations*. Spark360.com. https://portal.spark360.com/HealthyLiving/Health/All/9%20Ways%20to%20Reframe%20Negative%20Thoughts%20Into%20Positive%20Affirmations

Schnurr, L. N. (2019, September 24). *3 scientific studies that prove the power of positive thinking*. Medium. https://medium.com/swlh/3-scientific-studies-that-prove-the-power-of-positive-thinking-616477838555

Segerstrom, S. C., & Miller, G. E. (2004). Psychological stress and the human immune system: A meta-analytic study of 30 years of inquiry. *Psychological Bulletin*, *130*(4), 601–630. https://doi.org/10.1037/0033-2909.130.4.601

Singhal, M. (2019, May 23). *Develop positive attitude in children, learning, teaching kids to be more positive.* Www.parentcircle.com. https://www.parentcircle.com/how-to-develop-positive-attitude-in-children/article

Spielberg, S. (Director). (1975). *Jaws* [Film]. Zanuck/Brown Company; Universal Pictures.

Taylor, T. (2018, August 17). *The power of positivity for children - educationlearningtoys.com.* Educational, Learning, Development Toys and Games. https://educationlearningtoys.com/knowledge-base/the-power-of-positivity-for-children/

The importance of positive role models for children. (2016, November 11). Education and Behavior.

https://educationandbehavior.com/importance
-of-positive-role-models-for-children/

The Partnership for Drug-Free Kids. (2014, July 23).
*National study: Teens report higher use of performance
enhancing substances.* Www.prnewswire.com.
https://www.prnewswire.com/news-
releases/national-study-teens-report-higher-use-
of-performance-enhancing-substances-
268219362.html

Wagenhals, D. (2018, August 22). *Parents: Do you
understand your important power to reframe?* Lakeside.
https://lakesidelink.com/blog/diane-
wagenhals/parents-do-you-understand-your-
important-power-to-reframe/

Williams, E. (2018, May 29). *What is A growth mindset and
why it matters for children and their parents.* Third
Space Learning.
https://thirdspacelearning.com/blog/what-is-
growth-mindset/

www.ingramcontent.com/pod-product-compliance
Lightning Source LLC
LaVergne TN
LVHW051426080426
835508LV00022B/3257